NOELLE MO

MORE THAN
I'M SORRY
CARE GUIDE

KNOW MOORE CONSULTING

How To Help Any Mom
After the Loss of their Child
Using a Proven Step-by-Step Model

ISBN 978-1-939237-89-7

Published by Suncoast Digital Press, Inc.
Sarasota, Florida, U.S.A.

Credits: The Finley Project®

With permission and appreciation,
the graphics and materials of the model
which are included in this book
are original to The Finley Project®

https://www.thefinleyproject.org

Contents

This CARE GUIDE is based on and a companion to the book, also by Noelle Moore:

MORE THAN "I'M SORRY"

How to Help Any Mom

After the Loss of their Child,

Using a proven Step-by-Step Model

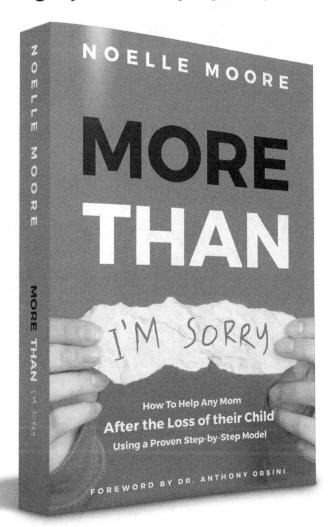

> "What does love look like? It has the hands to help others. It has the feet to hasten to the poor and needy. It has eyes to see misery and want. It has the ears to hear the sighs and sorrows of others. That is what love looks like."
>
> Saint Augustine

Leaves are timeless symbols of life, growth, protection, and renewal. In sacred text, they represent both fragility and durability; both hope and hardships. Through leaves, we receive oxygen. Let each leaf in this Care Guide give you energy and hope, just as you bring those to others.

MORE THAN "I'M SORRY"

How to BEST help in a Meaningful Way

Thank you for your concern, care, and commitment. The gratitude that a grieving mother and her family has for you is more than you can imagine. I speak on their behalf...I am one of them. I lost my daughter, Finley, when she was only three weeks old, and I've been healing ever since. In 2014, I founded The Finley Project, a nonprofit that has now helped hundreds of mothers after the loss of their child. The support and steps that have proven most useful are found in this Care Guide.

Proven Strategies and Steps: Actions to Take—Mistakes to Avoid

It may have happened suddenly, without any warning. Or you may have watched in agony as your sister, friend, neighbor, co-worker or other family member walked through the tearful journey of their child's illness. Each situation is different, but when someone you care about is hurting, you hurt, too.

Losing a child is nothing short of traumatic. It's nothing one can prepare for. Your heart aches for the grieving mom and you are desperate to help, but how? You and your friends, family, co-workers are feeling helpless, even useless, maybe even afraid to do the wrong thing, say the wrong thing. You want to offer something, more than words, more than "I'm Sorry."

WHO IS THIS CARE GUIDE FOR?

- You want to help a woman and her family get through the nightmare that no one should have to go through alone.

- You don't want to waste your own efforts and energy doing things that won't help much, if at all.

- You understand that the grieving mother does not know and cannot communicate what she needs.

- You want to know what having all the bases covered means and you are willing to ask others to cover them.

- You are eager to help others see exactly how they can best help, since many people are at a loss or afraid to do something that could make matters worse.

- You want to be educated and well-equipped now, even if the need is not imminent, so if something happens down the road you will be empowered to be a competent helper

- You are a leader who comes in contact with grieving families and wants a proven, life-changing tool to utilize in your role as a counselor, church or civic group leader, hospital administrator or chaplain, or grief support group leader.

- You commit to being the go-person, the central volunteer who will communicate to others what is needed, by when, and how to accomplish it (which is ALL right here in this book for you!).

This Care Guide is here to help and guide you with actionable steps you can take, knowing that our approach has helped many, many grieving mothers in meaningful ways.

Through this Care Guide, you will discover the essence of what is needed, understand the fundamentals of how to help, and learn the difference-making steps you can take, starting now. I designed it like a workbook or notebook, so you can easily keep everything written down, organized, and in one place.

The Finley Project Model® will be your powerful, effective, and highly specialized tool. There is no loss that this process cannot help—whether it is an infant loss, which is what this process was built upon, or an elderly grandparent, this model enables, equips and engages you with a grieving person through practical and physical support methods.

It's a great idea to invite others to partner with you to utilize these strategies. In fact, it's imperative. This multi-faceted approach needs a community, a team. given the nature of help needed. Most everyone is unaware with how to help and would appreciate actionable steps and ideas for the best way to be supportive of the grieving mother whom they care about. You can gather together, pool resources, and follow the process. So, please follow along to learn more how your family, friend group, civic group, coworkers, church congregation, synagogue, or neighborhood group can make a difference in helping someone who is in the throws of loss.

It's important to remember, "it's a marathon, not a sprint," when it comes to helping a person navigate through a painful loss. There is no one experience that defines "grief." Everyone goes through it differently, depending on their own belief system, their relationship with their deceased loved one, the strength of their personal resilience, and especially the support they have around them.

I will show you here why this unique, real-world Model which I developed matters, how much it costs to support a hurting person, and how to help, step-by-step.

> " *"Love and kindness are never wasted. They always make a difference. They bless the one who receives them, and they bless you, the giver."*
>
> Barbara De Angelis "

THE FINLEY PROJECT MODEL

What Others are Saying

"During this period of intense grief, Moore realized that there were very few holistic resources aimed at helping mothers get through the most catastrophic stages of loss, and decided to start an organization of her own, which became The Finley Project."

—People Magazine (May 18, 2021). "After Losing Their Own Babies, These Women Now Help Others Get Through 'Literally, Your Worst Nightmare'."

"I was in a really bad place and I didn't want to live any more. I wasn't leaving my house and I was a shell of a person. You lose yourself, but The Finley Project came in and brought me back to life. The cleanings helped me feel human again, the massages released tension, and the Counseling made me feel like my grief was normal. The meet-ups made me feel like I was in a safe place."

—Maria Felton, a mother in The Finley Project Program, lost her 10-month-old son, MJ

"The Finley Project has found a way to turn tragedy into beauty. Their devotion to grieving mothers is incredibly heartwarming and we are honored to be a part of the healing process. The benefits of massage are numerous especially when the recipient is in a state of grief. Grief is a prime contributor to stress and stress can have long-term effects on the body. Massage can assist with the physical and even emotional ramifications associated with grief."

—Erika and Michel Sasser, Owners, Massage Envy Spa®, Altamonte Springs, Florida

"The Finley Project helped in so many ways. The house cleaners were a blessing because I was recovering from emergency surgery. My husband had lost his job right before our loss so the gift cards for food helped keep us fed. I'm still seeing the amazing counselor they found for me and more than anything, The Finley Project helped me not feel so alone in all of this."

—Danielle Koch, a mother in The Finley Project Program, lost her daughter, Kaylin, during labor

The Finley Project Model - Why the Model Matters

Grief does strange things to people. It often creates a haze or fuzz over the brain. Grieving individuals are often unable to "think." Their brain processes simply do not function as usual because the pain is all consuming. According to Amy Paturel in her article "The Traumatic Loss of a Loved One Is Like Experiencing a Brain Injury" the brain function during grief is described in the following way:

> "In an attempt to manage overwhelming thoughts and emotions while maintaining function, the brain acts as a super-filter to keep memories and emotions in a tolerable zone or obliterate them altogether. According to a 2019 study published in Social Cognitive and Affective Neuroscience, grievers minimize awareness of thoughts related to their loss. The result: heightened anxiety and an inability to think straight." (https://www.discovermagazine.com/mind/the-traumatic-loss-of-a-loved-one-is-like-experiencing-a-brain-injury)

Inability to think straight. I know this to be true because I lived it. Also, I've personally supported many grieving people who were obviously in a daze or foggy state of mind. The Finley Project Model is based on this principle: Be the brain for the mother (or any person in the abyss of loss) who is unable to think for themselves. Take action, say "More than I'm Sorry" because the grieving person needs you.

The reason that this book and The Finley Project Model® is critical is that others in the grieving person's life need to help guide and direct their steps because they are simply not able to "think straight." And, they don't know what they need. They can't tell you how best to support them, but I will.

When someone experiences a loss, they are in it and feel every ounce of it sometimes, but other times they don't know what to feel, if anything, so they are lost. Those on the outside are able to support because they have more ability to think.

You may be grieving along with the mother. Maybe the lost child was your own, or a nephew, or granddaughter. However much you are hurting, the mom is in so, so much deeper pain… even when it doesn't seem that way. Only others can bring the clarity, strength, perspective and mental fortitude needed to develop plans and takes action. It's imperative that others come alongside a grieving person and be their eyes, ears, and mind—and then their "get it done" hands-on helpers. Everyone who wants to be of help starts with "I'm sorry" and those are caring words—but to really make a difference, both individuals and a support team will find this Care Guide essential to do "more than I'm sorry."

How Others can Help Others

OUR MISSION

The Finley Project is committed to providing care for mothers who have experienced the unimaginable — the loss of an infant. Our devoted team provides a lifeline for mothers in the minutes, hours and days after infant loss through a 7-Part Holistic Program that supports each mother physically, emotionally and spiritually at no financial cost to them.

@thefinleyproject

01. Help with Funeral Arrangements

02. Grocery Gift Cards

03. Professional House Cleaning

04. Professional Massage Therapy

05. Support Group Placement

06. One-on-One Professional Counseling

07. Support from a Volunteer Support Coordinator

The Finley Project Model®

The Finley Project Model® has been utilized through The Finley Project Program since 2013. It was developed to help mothers who lost an infant at any time between 22 weeks' gestation and two years of age. The Model has helped women who lost an infant due to various genetic issues, accidents, medical malpractice incidents, and other causes. (Sample: [Chart 1.1])

No	Date Enrolled	State	Condition/Reason
1	11/14/14	FL	Stillbirth
2	8/11/14	FL	Malpractice
3	1/7/15	NC	Hole in Heart
4	11/27/14	NC	Stillbirth
5	11/1/14	FL	Trisomy 18
6	9/23/14	FL	Stillbirth
7	4/27/15	FL	SIDS
8	5/14/15	FL	Stillbirth
9	4/24/15	FL	SIDS
10	8/7/15	FL	Cancer
11	9/28/15	FL	Stillbirth
12	10/26/15	NC	Cord Accident
13	10/18/15	FL	Encephala
14	3/6/15	CO	Premature
15	8/20/15	TX	Premature
16	1/4/16	FL	Premature
17	10/18/15	FL	Malpractice
18	6/30/15	NC	Campomelic Dysplasia
19	11/9//15	FL	Trisomy 18
20	1/29/16	FL	Stillbirth
21	11/16/15	FL	Stillbirth
22	2/16/16	FL	Premature
23	2/18/16	NC	Trisomy 18
24	2/15/16	LA	Congenial Heart Defect
25	4/16/16	MI	Stillbirth
26	4/13/16	PA	Krabbe Disease
27	4/26/16	NC	Stillbirth
28	4/27/16	NC	Premature
29	4/27/16	FL	Premature
30	5/10/16	WV	Trisomy 18

[Chart 1.1])

The Finley Project Model® was designed to "think for" the grieving mother when they couldn't think for themselves immediately after or shortly after the loss of a child. The Model also addresses the "whole" person—therefore, it is considered to be the nation's only Holistic Program for Mothers After Infant Loss. What makes The Finley Project Model stand out among other models is that it is all encompassing, where a person is assisted early with practical/physical needs being addressed and then the emotional/spiritual needs are being supported long-term.

When a death occurs, grief naturally takes over, but unfortunately the "to-do" list has just begun. The way The Finley Project Model® begins is by offering someone practical/physical support with a funeral, meal gift cards, and even house cleaning services. These initial things are very important for many reasons. By handling the practical needs, you are helping to ease physical burdens in the early days after loss.

The best "more than I'm sorry" support to provide is taking care of pressing tasks which are just too big a burden for a grieving mom or family. No one is prepared for this kind of loss. No "pre-planned funeral arrangements" have been set up, for example. The funeral planning support is something that most families can't even fathom having to deal with. By stepping in to handle logistics and helping to create honoring elements, stress is eased on the family.

Funeral Planning Support along with meal gift cards, house cleaning and massage therapy— allow those helping the grieving person the opportunity to gain or continue to build trust with the person they supporting. These are things that show one cares without requiring too much from the hurting person. This is love in action.

The long-term goal is to provide spiritual/emotional support through counseling and support group placement as well as connecting them to someone that has walked a similar journey — a dedicated support person. The initial practical/physical components help earn their trust and build loyalty while the spiritual/emotional components help provide tools and support for long-term healing.

The Finley Project Model is comprised of Seven Parts [Chart 1.2]:

1. AID: Planning the Funeral/Celebration of Life
2. NOURISH: Meal or Grocery Gift Cards
3. CLEANSE: House Cleaning   } Physical/Practical
4. RESTORE: Massage Therapy

5. COUNSEL: Licensed Mental Health Counseling
6. FELLOWSHIP: Support Group Placement   } Spiritual/Emotional
7. SUPPORT: Support from Volunteers

Let's Get Started!

Gather Your Helpers

Deciding on a leader defines your role and makes it easier for eager helpers to reach out to you. They don't want to bug the mom, her husband, her mother...they literally don't know who can tell them what is needed, and what they can do that would truly be supportive. As a person reading this Care Guide, you may be the one leading others into how to help. Go ahead and write the leader's name (perhaps your own) below.

MY NAME IS_____

As a mom who's been there, I must take this opportunity to say THANK YOU. You may understand that your efforts will help out a grieving mom you care about, but you can't imagine what a meaningful difference you are making. The journey is not going to be a bed of roses for anyone, and yet, right now you feel like this is something you want to take on. Why is that? Write down your "why" so that you can come back to it any time. Think about your intention, something that inspires you, the very thing that makes you want to help your hurting friend, co-worker, family or community member. The encourager needs encouragement, too!

MY INTENTION IS TO_____

_____SO THAT _____

_____

It's important to title your role and group and give people a sense that someone is organizing and managing things in a helpful, purposeful way—that when they decide to participate, it won't be chaotic and stressful. You can use the family's last name, for example, "Moore Support Team."

You will be collecting names, organizing task assignments, and managing your helpers.

The good news is that we at The Finley Project have been doing these things for years in order to support overwhelmed mothers who cannot think for themselves. Each step in the process has been improved again and again so your job can be accomplished as smoothly and effectively as possible. Alternative steps are included as well.

Use this Care Guide and the worksheets (which you may want to photocopy, take pictures of and text, etc) to help you and others stay organized. This Care Guide will give you confidence that you have all the bases covered, and to stay inspired and motivated in this role you've taken, making huge difference—not only for the grieving mother, but for her family and all the people who want to contribute in some way to support her.

Use the following worksheet to start your list.

GENERAL INFO

MOM'S ADDRESS	
MOM'S PHONE NUMBER	
CHILD'S NAME	
CHILD'S BIRTHDATE	
CHILD'S DAY OF DEATH	

_____ SUPPORT TEAM

(FAMILY NAME)

Assignment	NAME
Head Coordinator	
Funeral Planning Coordinator	
Gift Cards Coordinator	
House Cleaning Coordinator	
Massage Therapy Coordinator	
Support Group Placement Coordinator	
Counseling Coordinator	
Dedicated Support Person	

PHONE NUMBER	EMAIL	CITY of RESIDENCE	RELATION TO MOM

_____ **SUPPORT TEAM**
(FAMILY NAME)

OTHER Assignments	NAME

PHONE NUMBER	EMAIL	CITY of RESIDENCE	RELATION TO MOM

EACH OF THE 7 STEPS will be covered, and each will have various tasks and helpers matched to the assignments.

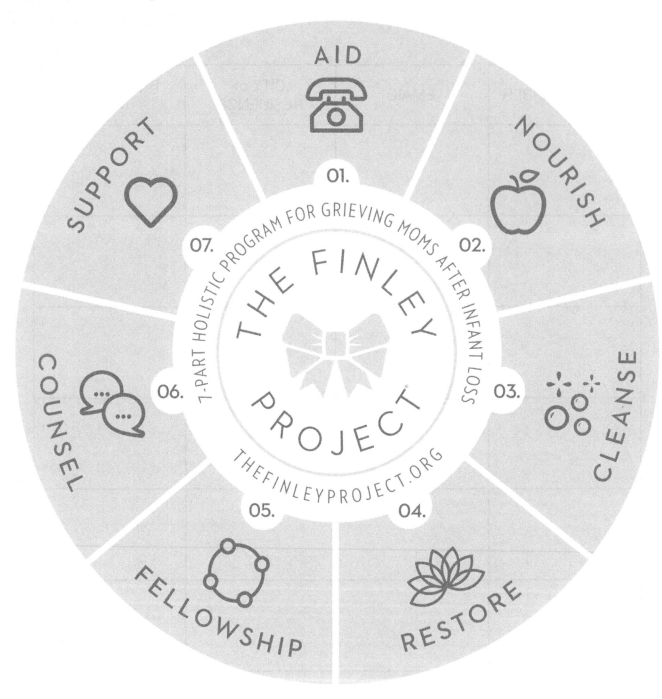

[Chart 1.2]

"I always ask God to work through me and let me be a light of some kind and help in this world, so I always pray for that, and I always want to do good."

Dolly Parton

The Finley Project Model® Cost Breakdown

Depending on the state, city, and other individual factors, the expenses herein are approximates based on our experience, but will undoubtedly rise with time. The costs, without funeral expenses, are approximately $1500. As seen through The Finley Project Model, the cost breakdown is as such:

The Finley Project: Cost per Mom w/Full Program Involvement			
Type of Support	Cost per day	Total days	Total costs
Professional Cleaning	$100.00	3	$300.00
Meal & Grocery Gift Cards	$25.00	7	$175.00
Licensed Mental Health Counseling	$70.00	12	$840.00
Massage Therapy	$60.00	3	$180.00
Total			$1,495.00
Cost to sponsor a mom			$1,495.00

The Overview of Cost should give those wanting to help an idea of what needs to be raised and collected in order to meet these critical needs. The costs vary based on locale and providers used, but these variances and alternatives will be discussed throughout each Step.

There are many ways to raise and gather support. Be creative and don't be afraid to ask! Be sure to highlight what the money raised is going to SPECIFICALLY. Some support raising suggestions:

- Gofundme or other internet-based fundraising platforms
- Car wash
- Bake sale or pancake breakfast
- Virtual silent auction (one resource is https://www.32auctions.com/)

As You Use This Care Guide...

Each Step explains the actions which our model has proven to be the most practical and helpful ways to support a grieving mom. Are there other things that can be done? YES! If one of the actions doesn't seem to fit your situation, look for alternatives to accomplish something that helps in that Step.

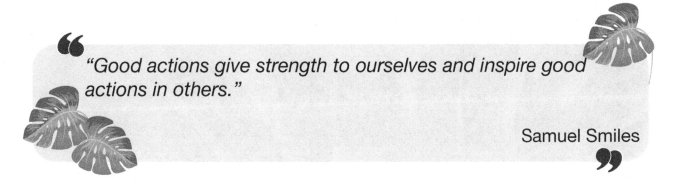

"*Good actions give strength to ourselves and inspire good actions in others.*"

Samuel Smiles

A tip while helping support:

The Head Coordinator doesn't have to be the only leader in the mission to help a grieving mom. Depending on the size of your group helping, you may need others to fill big and sometimes time-consuming roles. Everyone has the same goal of supporting the mother, but the way each person contributes and participates can be personal to them, and that's okay. Be sensitive to how your volunteers are responding and accomplishing their tasks. Be flexible and help people find ways to be supportive that also work for them.

19

(1)

AID

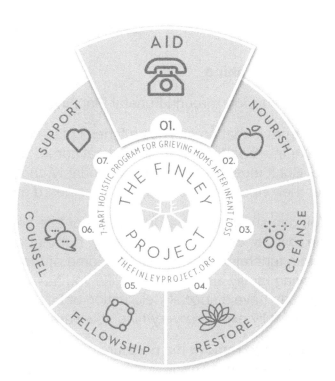

When you think of "AID," think "Assistance In Dealing." Helping and assisting someone after loss is why you are here and one way that this is helpful is helping with Funeral Planning. Just when a grieving mother feels like sleeping her day away or whatever gets her through each hour, she is going to be asked to make certain decisions. This is an area where you can step in and walk with her, assisting her through the Funeral Planning process.

> "An ask or pressure for any decision can feel extremely overwhelming. A mom doesn't know which way is up and needs AID in planning the hardest funeral she will ever attend. "
>
> Noelle Moore, a mom who's been there

Example of How to Help Aid:

Funeral Planning

Why is support through Funeral Planning important?

The truth is that no one has a funeral plan already set up for a little child. No one wants to make the dreaded call to the funeral home. Cute nursery at home, yes—funeral arrangements, no. But it must be done. Understandably, the parents are not in any condition to deal with this, yet their input and wishes need to be heard and honored.

You can suggest that a Celebration of Life be held at a later time, even a year or two down the road, or on the child's birthday, but that is just an option in contrast or in conjunction with a funeral shortly thereafter. Some of the most beneficial words I have ever shared with a grieving family are, "Don't feel like you have to do everything and anything during their funeral. You can have a special Celebration of Life in a year or two so you have time to plan it out and have it fully express everything you want. It's okay to wait to do something down the road."

You want to remove the pressure of trying to honor the deceased infant in every way which is overwhelming. This is not the end of this person's memory or honoring them. A helper can talk to a funeral home, relay the parents' wishes, set up the logistics.

What can you do?

For a more traditional "Funeral Ceremony:"

- Offer to help go through/create an outline of meaningful speakers, songs, "things" for the day.

- Offer to have a beautiful program created such as Cherished Prints – cherished-prints.com/shop/. These are customized programs that are beautifully put together.

- Offer to help plan the meal after the ceremony.

- Offer to help set up/plan an honor space/table.

NOTES

_____

_____

_____

_____

Alternative:

For a "Celebration of Life:"

- Offer to plan the event – i.e., BBQ, nice dinner, get-together.

- Set up the food – catering, potluck, cooking on site, etc.

- Offer to help go through/create an outline of meaningful speakers, songs, "things" for the day.

- Offer to have a beautiful program created such as Cherished Prints – cherished-prints.com/shop/. These are customized programs that are beautifully put together.

- Offer to purchase butterflies for a release or lanterns.

- Offer an Honor Space/table. This space can include pictures, favorite items, memories. One idea that's special is to have rocks laid out and guests sign the rocks. The rocks can then be placed in a container of placed in a garden.

NOTES

_____

_____

_____

_____

_____

_____

_____

_____

_____

Checklist:

Name of Person Assigned to Coordinate Funeral Plans: _____

Funeral or Celebration of Life Location: _____

Burial or Cremation: _____

Funeral Date: _____

Guest List Assigned To: _____

Event Invite Created (social media): _____

Songs Selected: _____

Format (speakers, songs, open mic): _____

Program Created (if so, by whom): _____

Items for Remembrance Table Gathered: _____

Food/Caterer: _____

NOTES

_____

_____

_____

_____

_____

NOTES

(2)
NOURISH

Like an extremely wilted plant, a grieving mom is in dire need of nourishment. It's not that hard to provide, but don't expect her to recognize how much she needs it. A grieving mother is not typically worried about food or eating. She doesn't care; she is wilting away and needs help.

Example of How to Help Nourish:

Meal Delivery & Grocery Gift Cards

Why are Meal & Grocery Gift Cards Important?

When I first started The Finley Project, I remember being eager to offer counseling to families. However, after my daughter Finley's death, the first family I knew to lose an infant was not open to counseling right away. The mother said, "I appreciate your willingness to help me and get me into counseling, but I can't even think about that right now. I had to stay in a Ronald McDonald house while my child was in the NICU for 3 months. Now I'm home and I have to manage my household pretty much by myself? I can barely get food on the table or have the money to buy groceries. I just need some basic help first."

A light went off for me then. I realized that people need to feel safe, secure, and cared for within their home first before they can engage in counseling. It became clear that The Finley Project needed to help the family first with the basics, including food.

A mother in The Finley Project program shared, "I received the gift cards. This was so appreciated by our family since dinner time is not the best time anymore. I've lost a lot of my interest in cooking since my daughter died…You are an amazing group of people. I hope to one day help a woman in this situation like you do. Thank you for your generosity and support!"

A lot of people decide to bring food to a grieving family which is a wonderful gesture. This can be done utilizing a scheduling platform such MeatItrain.com. This platform allows others to sign up for various meals and days. When doing this, please let the grieving family know this is being done and also that you will ask those doing the meals to leave the food in a place by the front door or on the porch (like in a large cooler).

Most grieving people do not want to have to socialize or "welcome" people into their home right after loss. It's important to let those know who are delivering food that their generous and caring hearts are appreciated, but the family is not yet ready for visitors. People may actually feel relieved that all they need to do is drop off the food, that more is not expected.

> "A well-meaning person needs to know the mom may not yet be ready to receive in-person words of sympathy or a hug. Please don't take it personally. It's like having a bad sunburn- and she needs space to heal."
>
> Noelle Moore, a mom who's been there

Another option if meals are not something that can be done, is to purchase grocery gift cards. The Finley Project found that Target or Walmart Gift cards were most helpful as it allowed families to purchase food, toiletries or other items. Other options for Gift Cards include – pizza delivery, fast food, Uber Eats, or local restaurants that deliver. Often families do not feel like getting out but are happy to have a meal delivered. Gift cards are a wonderful option even if there is a Mealtrain set up as it allows families to use them to go where they want to go or have what they want to have delivered on their own time. A mother in The Finley Project program shared,

> "I received the gift cards. This was so appreciated by our family since dinner time is not the best time anymore. I've lost a lot of my interest in cooking since my daughter died and now losing another child, it is very rare when I cook dinner anymore. You guys are an amazing group of people. I hope to one day help a woman in this situation…"
>
> A mom who received our "Nourishment"

Restaurant and grocery gift cards ensure that every mother and her family have hot meals and a stocked refrigerator.

Alternative:

Plan a less formal schedule for the long haul, by assigning a few friends, over 3 months, to bring a large meal, one time a week to remind the family they are cared for and loved. Providing a meal, once a week, allows a family to have leftovers and eat on the meal for a few days. This longer-term approach also provides food after others may have stopped providing meals.

NOTES

_____

_____

_____

_____

_____

Checklist:

Name of Person Assigned to Coordinate & Purchase Gift Cards: _____

Grieving Person's Preference - Target, Walmart or Other? _____

Gift Card Purchased & Given to the Grieving Person? _____

Cost for the Gift Card? _____

NOTES

_____

_____

_____

_____

_____

_____

_____

_____

_____

_____

_____

NOTES

(3)
CLEANSE

> "A clean and ordered environment helps a grieving mom begin to order her own internal space."
>
> Noelle Moore, a mom who's been there

Example of How to Help Cleanse:

House Cleaning

Why is House Cleaning Important?

As a mother grieves, simple daily tasks like cooking and cleaning are overwhelming. Housekeeping services provide a clean and healthy environment, but also relieve a burden or guilt/ pressure to do what she used to keep up with easily.

A family member or close friend can help just by getting all the piled-up dishes and kitchen cleaned, or fold all the laundry, or make the mother's bathroom sparkle. Anything helps.

Sometimes a mom prefers a stranger to do the cleaning—she doesn't want to feel embarrassed or uncomfortable. Ask if she's ever used a maid or cleaning service she liked. Pay for them to come. Or, hire a service you are familiar with and trust. You want to be certain this is stress-free for the mom. Take her to lunch or to a quite lake/park while her house is getting cleaned if you like.

VERY IMPORTANT NOTE: Do not take it upon yourself or let anyone touch the child's belongings or remove any "sad memories." The grieving mom must have control over this process. It can do more harm than good to not respect this.

Taylor Gat, a Program mother shared, "We had all of Benjamin's toys out in the living room since that's where we spent most of our time together. We left everything untouched for probably a month and then I decided it was time to put things away. We had people offer to help, but I felt like this was something I needed to do on my own as part of my grieving. I felt like if we allowed someone else to do that, we wouldn't process that part of him being gone."

Another Program mother Joanna Lynch shared, "While I was at the hospital, I had a friend go stay with my pets. I asked her to box everything up and put it away before I got home. I thought it would be too hard to see it. This was a huge mistake. A few others came over and cleared my son's room out completely and ended up putting his stuff in the attic. Coming home to an empty room and knowing his stuff was up there killed me. I made my husband go up and take it all back down. It's still in boxes in his closet and I still like to go in there and sit in the recliner and hold some of his things. I don't really plan on ever getting rid of it. I hope one day I can share it with a sibling of his and use it to remember him by."

Erica Dameron, received the terrible news that her child would not be born alive, yet she had to go through the birthing process. Months later, she said, "While I was at the hospital waiting to give birth to my daughter, Peyton, I had some friends offer to go to my house and pack up her room. This infuriated me. I hadn't even given birth to her yet and people were wanting to erase her from my house. I know they were just trying to be helpful, but it was extremely hurtful. Once I got home, I didn't really touch her things for a few months."

Another Program mom, Elizabeth Romero, told us, "I keep some of her items in my closet, right next to my stuff. It's a daily reminder of her and brings me comfort to see her little shoes and onesie next to my clothes. Her stuff reminds me she existed and is my child, even if she never got to wear them."

If you are rather surprised to know how some mothers feel about their child's belongings, you are not alone. How could you guess this? Many moms say that people incorrectly assume that the things which trigger memories of the child should be out of sight. As one mom put it, "Why? Do they think I would completely forget this ever happened? As if hiding a car seat or little blanket would allow me to forget?"

This process can sometimes take months if not years to walk through.

The Cleanse Step is therefore *not the task of cleaning out a deceased child's things*; it is for handling any typical cleaning and organizing that the mother would normally be able to do. This Step helps the mom in many ways—it can give her a sense that there's order.

To offer cleaning, all logistics will need to be handled. Assuming she does not already use or know of a cleaning company she wants, you or your helper will need to find one.

"*It is proven that an important part of a grieving person's healing process is going through the deceased loved one's belongings when they are ready.* "

Noelle Moore, a mom who's been there

Here are some suggestions when starting the process of figuring out cleaning for the grieving person:

Is there a national chain in their area? Why a national chain?

- They are licensed/ insured and make a person feel more comfortable then a local company.

- They often work with organizations that handle complex medical issues and can be more sensitive to what you are trying to do.

Tips when dealing with National Cleaning Companies:

- They often don't work on the weekends or at night.

- Don't be afraid to tell them that the cleaning is for someone that lost a child or loved one. Feel free to let them know the person may be very sensitive to items in the home that they would not like touched. For example: We once had a mother who lost her 2-year-old daughter who, on her last day alive, had placed her sticky little hands on the sliding glass doors. This mother requested the glass not be cleaned.

- Another example: A mother had been breastfeeding her premature baby while in the NICU, but once he died, the mother left all the bottles, bottle brush and breast pump in a certain place on the counter. She asked that the cleaning company not move or touch these items as that was the last place, she had left it before her son died.

- Let them know you would like three 1-hour cleanings over the course of three months.

- Ask if the mother or grieving person can call and ask questions about what can and can't be cleaned.

- They will need a credit card on file.

- Make sure the day before, you confirm the appointment and payment info is on file! This is important!

Tips when dealing with the grieving mother or person for cleaning:

- Find out if there is a day of the week that is best. Weekends and nights are not typically options.

- Scheduled the same day and time over three months. Remember – it's about the long haul!

- Let the mother or grieving person know they can call the cleaning company and ask questions about what can and can't be cleaned.

Some of the mothers felt a sense of relief with their cleanings. Ashely Schimmer shared after her son Lincoln died:

> "The cleaning ladies just did an amazing, fantastic job as always! Thank you so very much. Having a clean home is so I nice. It is hard finding motivation to go dust, mop, etc., the whole house, but specifically…in the nursery. One of the cleaning ladies, who has been cleaning since the first visit, offered to mop and dust in my baby Lincoln's room today. ☺ It made my heart so happy! I got to show off his room and pictures. It made me burst with pride getting to talk about our Lincoln. She really went above and beyond! Walking inside my house from getting my daughter, it smelled so nice and fresh! After dreading Mother's Day this last week leading up to it and the lack of motivation for anything, my house greatly suffered. Having one less thing to worry about is such a relief! Thank You Thank you."

Alternative:

If a professional service cannot be afforded, an option would be to gather a few friends together to clean the home for the person. This sometimes works as long as the person doesn't feel judged or uncomfortable. Sometimes a stranger (an outside cleaning company) is the best option as there is less room for shame/embarrassment. Other times, a group of friends helps to ease any uncomfortable feelings or uncertainty about a stranger in their home. Whoever is helping must be clear about the grieving mom's wishes such as whether something should be moved or touched at all.

> *"No act of kindness, no matter how small, is ever wasted."*
>
> Aesop

NOTES

_____

_____

_____

_____

_____

Checklist:

Name of Person Assigned to Coordinate & Schedule Housecleaning: _____

Cleaning Location Phone Number & Contact: _____

Cost per Cleaning: _____

Dates Scheduled:

    1. _____

    2. _____

    3. _____

Has the Information been communicated to the Grieving Person? _____

Did the Grieving Person place the dates/times on a calendar? _____

NOTES

_____

_____

_____

_____

_____

_____

_____

NOTES

(4)
RESTORE

"My heart felt broken and my body, too. I needed help being put back together...I needed to be restored. Massage therapy allowed me meaningful moments to feel like a whole person again. To feel worthy of time and touch made me feel more me again."

Noelle Moore, a mom who's been there

Example of How to Help Restore:

Massage Therapy

Why is Massage Therapy Important?

> *"The benefits of massage are numerous especially when the recipient is in a state of grief. Grief is a prime contributor to stress and stress can have long-term effects on the body. Massage can assist with the physical and even emotional ramifications associated with grief."*
>
> Erika and Michel Sasser, Owners, Massage Envy Spa

I laid on the massage table, under the warm blanket, in the low-light space of serenity. For the first time in a month, I felt a sense of peace. The first time I had a massage after Finley died was the first time that an entire sixty minutes passed and I had not cried. Massage brought a sense of calm to my aching heart and an hour of rest that often wasn't possible during sorrow-filled nights.

Consider the five main health benefits of massage therapy according to the American Massage Therapy Association (AMTA). It is clear that each one of these are perfect ways to help a grieving mother.

1. Lowers stress—The effects of stress can take emotional and physical tolls. Massage therapy can relieve stress and conditions associated with it, such as tension headaches.

2. Increase immune function—Massage therapy can help boost immune system strength.

3. Boost mental health and wellness—Symptoms of stress, anxiety and depression (all associated with mental health) may be directly affected with massage therapy.

4. Manage pain—Pain can negatively affect a person's quality of life and impede recovery from illness or injury.

5. Improve physical fitness—Massage can reduce muscle tension, improve exercise performance and prevent injuries.

Remember, a grieving person is not capable of thinking, so your role is to think for them. You can ask the mom to choose three dates over the next one-to-three months that work for them. You or another helper can handle booking the appointments directly with the licensed massage provider. Be sure to pay in advance, including a gratuity, and remind the provider that all they need to say when their client checks out is "It's all taken care of."

What you can do?

The Finley Project Model provides three massage sessions that are given once a month for three months. The Finley Project Model uses   a licensed national massage chain that is reputable and insured for comfortability.

In order to ensure the grieving person enjoys the full benefit of Massage over the duration of the few months following their loss, booking the appointments, all at the same time, is helpful. Remember, a grieving person is not capable of thinking, so your role is to "think for them." You can ask the person for 3 dates, over the next 3 months that work for them and you book them directly with the Massage provider. When calling, you can let them know the following:

- You are calling on behalf of someone that has experienced a significant loss

- You are looking to book three massage appointments over three months for them

- You will be responsible for paying for the service AS well as gratuity. Please remind them that you do not want them asking for payment from the person at check-out.

- The Massage chain may ask you to complete a Credit Authorization form electronically, if so complete and send back.

- If the Massage chain does not ask you to complete the form, you will be asked for payment over the phone. If you are comfortable do so, you can provide it at that time.

- You will need to provide the person's phone number along with last name.

- Once the appointments are booked, let the person know they have appointments scheduled and where the location is. Have the person plug the info into their calendar or phone. Let the person know they will need to arrive 15 mins early to their appointment to fill out paperwork and that they should not be asked to pay anything at the end of their session.

The average cost for massage therapy at a national chain is $50 for the first appointment for a new client, then a tip on top of the service of $12-$15 is recommended. After that, the 2nd and 3rd massages often cost more, around $80-$90 a session, plus tip $12-$15 tip. In total, the cost for the three massages over a three months' time will cost your tribe approximately $255-$275.

Alternative:

If a regular Massage Therapist or Spa is not an option due to cost, an alternative solution is a Massage Therapy School. Often these schools are good for those in training and offer low-cost options. Another option is to utilize "Groupon" who often offers significantly discounted massage sessions with great, qualified therapist looking for business.

Checklist:

Name of Person Assigned to Coordinate & Schedule Massages: _____

Massage Location Phone Number & Contact _____

Cost per Massage PLUS tip: _____

Dates Scheduled:

    1. _____

    2. _____

    3. _____

Has the Information been communicated to the Grieving Person? _____

Did the Grieving Person place the dates/times on a calendar? _____

NOTES

_____

_____

_____

_____

_____

_____

_____

NOTES

5
FELLOWSHIP

"Many mothers feel alone, like they are the only ones feeling such deep pain and loss. Connecting a mother to a community of others going through similar losses, can help greatly."

Noelle Moore, a mom who's been there

Example of Fellowship Support:

Support Group Placement

Why is a Support Group Important?

Feeling like she is not alone and is not the only one in the abyss of loss is critical for surviving, short-term and long-term.

Hope. The reason that being with others and hearing their stories, their ways of coping (or maybe not coping in some instances), is imperative is that this offers perspective and hope.

Some mothers worry that hearing about others' grief would be overwhelming, or that talking about their story would be too triggering to their own pain. The fact it that once a mother shows up and give a support group a try, most of them come back. Support groups are a safe space and create a sense of community. Mothers gather together with those rare people who have a real understanding of their particular kind of pain and grief. They find that in that group, they can share and be vulnerable. Support groups reveal the unspoken things women and men are going through.

Some groups are virtual, others are in-person. Some are "drop in" groups where a mother/father can attend at any time, while other groups are "closed" groups where one must register and attend for a set amount of weeks. Then those group sessions are complete and usually a new group becomes open for both people who want to re-register as well as new participants.

A wonderful, weekly, in-person, closed group is GriefShare (www.griefshare.com), a support group program, that saved my life. The reason this group was so valuable was that it made me feel less alone and had a 13-week curriculum with action steps. In my particular group, the leaders were incredible as they greeted me with love and compassion. I can remember arriving to the church where the support group was located and could barely walk in. I was scared. However, instead of sitting back and waiting for the attendees to enter, the group leaders, Dale and Elaine Coulter, were waiting outside the room, welcoming me and directing me where to go. The comfort and peace these two life-saving leaders provided made me want to come back and participate.

Another group, The Compassionate Friends provides hope and understanding to those who have lost a child at any age due to any cause. https://www.compassionatefriends.org/

Other Support group options include Virtual groups. Virtual Groups have the benefit of convenience. Mothers usually don't feel up to driving themselves anywhere and there may not be easy transportation options for her. If you suggest a local group and she declines, ask her about a virtual one because that may be a good solution.

VIRTUAL SUPPORT GROUP FOR
PREGNANCY AND INFANT LOSS
(up to age 1)

- **M.E.N.D. (Mommies Enduring Neonatal Death)** is a Christian, non-profit organization that reaches out to families who have suffered the loss of a baby through miscarriage, stillbirth, or early infant death. M.E.N.D. is a place for families to connect, share their unique story of loss, and learn to live life without your precious baby.
https://www.mend.org/

- **M.E.N.D. Nationwide Online Support Group** is a Christian, non-profit organization that reaches out to families who have suffered the loss of a baby through miscarriage, stillbirth, or early infant death. The group is on the third Thursday of each month at 8:00 p.m. Central.
https://www.mend.org/nationwide-online-support-group

- **Share Pregnancy and Infant Loss Support** is a community for anyone in the family who has experienced the tragic loss of a baby.
http://nationalshare.org/online-support/

- **Star Legacy Foundation Online Support Group** provides live, online support groups for families who have experienced a perinatal loss. Groups are held via HIPAA-compliant videoconferencing and facilitated by trained health professionals. Registration is required only for the first time you attend.
https://starlegacyfoundation.org/support-groups/

- **TEARS Foundation** offers free support groups for bereaved families who have experienced the death of their baby. The groups are always open monthly to new members, and everyone is welcome to attend. Support for the deaf community and Spanish speaking community is also available.
https://thetearsfoundation.org/

NOTES

_____

_____

_____

_____

_____

SUPPORT GROUPS FOR DEATH OF A CHILD AT ANY AGE:

- **Bereaved Parents of the USA** provides a safe space where grieving parents and families can rebuild their lives after the death of a child. https://www.bereavedparentsusa.org/

- **MISS Foundation** provides services to families who have experienced the death of a child at any age. https://missfoundation.org/. They provide a free, 24/7, fully moderated online support group forums. Their moderators are fully trained and are also bereaved parents, grandparents, or siblings themselves. If you would like to join the forums, you'll need to apply for membership which will take 24 to 78 hours before it clears. If you'd like to apply to join the online support group: https://forums.missfoundation.org/login/

SUPPORT GROUP FOR Sudden Infant Death Syndrome (SIDS) and other sleep-related infant death:

- **First Candle** offers online support groups for those who have experienced loss by Sudden Infant Death Syndrome, stillbirth and miscarriage.

SUPPORT GROUP FOR
Sudden Unexplained Death in Childhood (SUDC)
A category of death in children between the ages of 1 and 18 years that remains unexplained after a thorough investigation, including an autopsy. Most often, a seemingly healthy child goes to sleep and never wakes up:

- **SUDC Foundation** offers resources and support for bereaved families who lost children due to sudden unexplained death.

NOTES

_____

_____

_____

_____

_____

Here is an **online support community** that focus on **children's grief**:

- **The National Alliance for Children's Grief (NACG)** is a nonprofit organization that raises awareness about the needs of children and teens who are grieving a death and provides education and resources for anyone who supports them. Through the collective voice of our members and partners, we educate, advocate, and raise awareness about childhood bereavement. https://childrengrieve.org/

Hospice Organizations – Hospice organizations have a variety of Support Groups for different types of losses.

Hospitals – Many hospitals have groups especially for those who have lost an infant or young child. Be sure to check ALL area hospitals, not just the one where the person was admitted, as groups are typically open to all people.

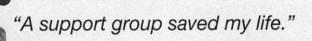

"A support group saved my life."

Noelle Moore, a mom who's been there

Alternative:

If a Support Group is not available in the person's area, one of the best options is an online support group. Can't find one you think would be a good match? Organize one by using social media or connecting with hospice social workers, grief counselors, or church leaders.

NOTES

_____

_____

_____

_____

_____

_____

Checklist:

Person Assigned to Coordinate Support Groups: _____

Support Group Suggested: _____

Support Group Address & Leader Contact Information: _____

_____

Support Group Day/Time Meeting: _____

Length of Support Group? Or Drop In: _____

Information communicated to the grieving person? _____

Other Support Group Suggested: _____

Support Group Address & Leader Contact Information: _____

_____

Support Group Day/Time Meeting: _____

Length of Support Group? Or Drop In: _____

Information communicated to the grieving person? _____

NOTES

6
COUNSEL

Example of Support through Counsel:

Licensed Mental Health Counseling

Why is Licensed Mental Health Counseling important?

Licensed Mental Health Counseling is the piece in supporting someone that is most important for their long-term health. Counseling is important long-term because the counselor becomes a person's go-to support system for the months and years to come. Family and friends can only provide support as their own work, proximity, and obligations allow. Counselors fill in the large gaps where others cannot and, most importantly, they are trained to address the intense psychological effects of having a child pass away.

Angela Sanders, a mother in The Finley Project Program lost her son Milo in 2016 to stillbirth. She shared how counseling helped her:

> "The Finley Project helped me from the beginning. Noelle texted support the day of my son's funeral and it was so helpful to hear from someone who had survived. I desperately needed someone to tell me how to keep living and The Finley Project helped me kickstart a healthy direction. Counseling saved my life, my marriage, and made me feel less alone."

The Finley Project Counseling Philosophy:

The Finley Project directs mothers to counseling providers immediately after a mother experiences the loss of an infant up to 90 days after loss. The Finley Project program directs and pays for counseling support that functions in the following ways:

- Counseling is provided as soon as possible to a mother, either through paying in full for sessions or paying for co-pays if the mother has an insurance benefit.

- Counseling is structured in such a way that it is intensive at first, 12 sessions weekly, then moves to a less frequent process after these initial 12 sessions. The initial 12 are paid for by The Finley Project. Next steps are to be determined by the counselor and mother after this period.

- Counseling services serve as a safeguard. Counselors provide the only clinical oversight for mothers in The Finley Project program. The Finley Project is the "concierge" in the process, coordinating the support and payment for the mothers for the counseling.

To help your grieving mother, this step is the one where you need to be persistent and persuasive. Yes, earlier steps must be addressed to help stabilize her home, but then she needs professional help. She may not agree. Here are some of the objections you may hear:

- "I don't need a counselor"

- "I've gone before, and it doesn't help"

- "I don't like my counselor"

- "I don't even know where to begin."

- "I can't afford it."

Help her find a counselor who has a lot of experience under his/her belt. Grief experience is a plus, such as if the counselor has lead grief support groups before, has counseled those going through grief, etc. There are some counselors that specialize in grief, but it's not a requirement. Tell the mom that all she must do is show up, she does not need to know how or what to talk about—the counselor will make her feel comfortable and lead the process.

Help her check with her insurance company to see what may be covered. Make a plan with the Support team to raise funds to cover what more is needed for at least three months. Also, check around in her community for free counseling offered through churches, colleges, and other organizations.

Questions you may have are listed below:

A.   Are there counselors that specialize in grief?

"The short answer is yes, there is training and certifications that will give you the title of a "Certified Grief Counselor". It looks great on a resume, but certainly, in my opinion, not necessary. The longer answer is more complex. What you want to look for in a good grief counselor is a highly trained therapist that has the skills and tools to deal with the trauma of loss, which is complicated and messy. You need a counselor that is not afraid of death and a heartache that is so deep that Mothers feel it physically. You need a counselor that understands that the loss of a child is just not overwhelming in the present, but also devastates the vision of the future that had been dreamed of for their child. Trying to find meaning in the chaos of losing a child also connects to the past and can make both parents second guess every pregnancy decision and life choice to try to ascribe meaning to the loss. A good counselor will be able to hold and explore the past, present and future at the same time, while also instilling hope that the depth of what they feel today will not be what they feel forever. Grief is a very complicated journey and each mother needs to be treated as an individual and not a "process" that she has to get through. The beauty of The Finley Project is that we are caring for not only Mom but the whole family. When Mom has a safe place to mourn, she can be more present with the rest of her family. She is also able to give space to others in the household whose grief might look different than hers, such as the non-birthing parent not showing pain to her because they feel they have to remain strong for the family, or even other children who don't understand what has happened. Having the skills to navigate, without fear, the convoluted, painful and sometimes chaotic state that is grief is what makes a good grief counselor." Chris Kavenagh, LMHC, www.FiveStonesCounseling.com

NOTES

_____

_____

_____

_____

_____

_____

B.   Should a mother's husband go? Or her significant other go to counseling?

In 2014, I met a young woman from South Florida, who was hesitant on going to counseling and asked if her boyfriend could attend with her. I let he know that in our program, we like to mothers to attend the first two to three sessions on their own, and then the spouse, significant other can join. This particular mother understood and went to the first counseling session. It was after that session, that the mother disclosed she was having major relational issues with her boyfriend and she was thankful to have a safe place to share with her counselor.

Although this is certainly not the case for everyone, it is often true that relationship tensions are high after child loss or loss in general. Whether verbalized or not, grieving people often feel that counseling offers a safe place to work through dealing with spouses, family members and significant others without judgement or conservation.

There are many instances on the flipside, where spouses and partners help each other immensely by going together. They have the chance to hear each other share and express things in a safe space to the counselor which they were hesitant to ask their partner about. If appropriate and helpful, it is certainly okay for couples to go together to work through the loss.

C.   She has insurance, can this be used for counseling?

Insurance coverage for counseling is very tricky, but there are ways you can help. First and foremost, have the mother call her insurance company and find out about her insurance benefits. Some coverage includes only a few "free" sessions, while others cover an unlimited amount with a small copay. There is also coverage that provides sessions 100% at no charge. Once a mother finds this information out, ask her to find a list of providers in her area that accepts that type of insurance. She should be able to go online to her insurance providers website to find these providers. From there, you could help by calling to see if they are taking new clients and if they have someone on staff that has worked with family's experiencing loss.

NOTES

_____

_____

_____

_____

_____

D. A Grieving Person doesn't have insurance and we don't know where to begin?

One of the best places to begin is by asking around locally, seeing what you can find out through word-of-mouth. You may learn that there are counselors that others have used that may be willing to help at a discounted rate given the situation, or have a "sliding scale" fee structure to assist those with financial challenges. Another option is to ask on social media if anyone knows a counselor that has experience dealing with Grief and Loss. What this looks like is someone who has spent time working in the field, not just textbook training. It is important to select someone that has had the opportunity to work with many families and people experiencing grief. Typically, females like to work with females and males like to work with male therapists. If it is a couple attending counseling, a male or female can be appropriate. If word of mouth or social media is not helpful, start researching Licensed Mental Health Counselors (LMHC) in your area. You can reach out via email or call to see if they are accepting new patients. If they are accepting new patients, it's important to share with them what your group is trying to do and who you are in relation to the person you are trying to help. From there, you will want to discuss cost and availability. Questions to ask:

- Do you have nights/ weekends available?

- What is your typical cost per session?

- Is there any flexibility in your price per session? *

- Is there paperwork you can send ahead of time?

- Is there a credit card authorization form I need to complete since payment will not be covered by the client?

Alternative:

Often churches provide support with a resource of lay people who are trained through a nonprofit organization, Stephens Ministries. These are people who have a heart for the hurting and who do not charge anything. Also, some colleges, seminaries, and online universities have therapeutic counseling students in training that need hours. This may be an option also in your area.

NOTES

_____

_____

_____

_____

_____

Checklist:

Person Assigned to Coordinate and Schedule Counseling: _____

Availability of Counselor: Nights? Weekends? _____

Availability of Counselor: Weekdays? _____

Availability of Grieving Person: Nights? Weekends? _____

Availability of Grieving Person: Weekdays? _____

Cost per session? $ _____

Informed the Grieving Person about their first Appointment? _____

Grieving Person scheduled the next appointment? _____

NOTES

_____

_____

_____

_____

_____

_____

_____

_____

NOTES

7
SUPPORT

> "Start where you are. Use what you have. Do what you can."
>
> Arthur Ashe

Example of Support:

Dedicated Support Person

Why is a Dedicated Support Person Important?

The Support Coordinator or Supportive person provides attention and compassion, two elements vital to healing from a tragic loss. This person is the primary listening ear and gives much-needed encouragement and a shoulder to lean on. A Support person is ideally someone who has experienced a similar loss as that builds trust and repour that the support is coming from an experienced place.

A Dedicated Support person's job is not to press the grieving mother to look at the good that may one day come from her loss, nor to insist that she "move on with her life." The role is to simply have and share a confident attitude that she will get through this and that there is hope and life after loss. The Support person is probably not a professional or someone with "all the answers." Rather, they are a heart-to-heart listener and helper who can stand and say, "I made it, you can too."

When someone loses a child, there are often well-meaning family and friends around. The faces are familiar, but the mother knows that unless personally experienced, no one truly understands what it feels like to lose their own small child.

It may be that the best Support person would be a woman who has walked through this same kind of grief before. Losing a child is not a typical loss, no matter what anyone thinks. The feelings associated with grief like intense sadness, hurt, anger, and despair are amplified to a level that is scary. It's a deep despair that is so unfamiliar that it is hard to see out of. When a grieving mother meets someone who has a similar experience, all of these feelings feel less scary because they share a commonality with someone else. They feel less ostracized and alone because their feelings are often validated and affirmed by another. This cohesive connection helps a grieving person take steps forward, knowing that they are not abnormal for feeling such intense pain and that they can make it with the help of someone else.

The Finley Project was blessed to have some amazing women who have gone through the tragedy of losing a child including Jerilyn Hughes-Lorch. Jerilyn is a very special woman as she has dedicated her life to helping others after losing her daughter Kristina in 1978. For 20+ years, Jerilyn has poured her heart into women all over the country by sharing her story. Jerilyn shared with us about serving as a Volunteer Support Coordinator: "I hope to prepare moms for the unexpected emotions, especially in the first year. Each mother walks their own unique path and I hope to help them in that journey while honoring their precious angel."

One mother, Parecia DeGuzman explains, "After losing Elin, my Support Coordinator was the first person I talked to who actually understood what I felt. I had heard all the clichés from everyone else, but when we started talking, I felt peace! She seemed to read my mind, and express all that I was feeling, but trying to contain. She also convinced me to finally go to counseling, which ultimately saved my life."

How to find this person? Ask around for someone that has experienced a similar loss. Call your local church or synagogue and ask if they have a Grief Support group and contact its leader. You can even turn to social media to share a general request for someone who has experienced a specific type of loss that your friend/family is going through.

I will never forget how Lane Alexander supported me in my darkest time. She had been a friend I knew since high school whom I later played collegiate volleyball with, becoming one of my closest friends and still is to this day. Lane was at the hospital when Finley took her last breath and was there for me at my home, bringing me meals and checking on me.

Lane did something extraordinary, something I still cherish every time I see it. Lane reached out to me EVERY single 25th day of each month since Finley died. It was something simple such as "Thinking of you today" and included a pink bow or a little girl emoji. This commitment to follow up has made me feel less alone and not forgotten. I am so thankful that Lane has never, ever forgotten my Finley.

Note the importance of both immediate/short-term support and on-going long-term support. Never hesitate to reach out when the thought occurs, but you definitely want to pull together a supportive group to make sure there is consistency. For example, you could set a calendar reminder on your phone to remind you to make the phone call, send a "thinking of you" card, or even a simple, caring text message. Share this idea with others who want to be supportive throughout those first extremely challenging weeks and months.

NOTES

_____

_____

_____

_____

_____

_____

_____

What to look for in a supportive person?

- "Find someone in like shoes" What does this mean? if the person you are trying to find help for lost a toddler due to a drowning, you will want to find someone similar. Conversely, if the person you are supporting made a decision to have a medical termination in utero, you will want to find someone who has walked the road of a medical termination.

- "Time is NOT Indication of a healthy supportive person" – You and your group will need to check a supportive person's stability and where they are in their processing. Just because a person lost a child years ago, does not mean they are in a healthy space to support someone else.

- "Be up front and honest" – When asking a support person if they can help someone else, don't shrink back from the grieving person's story. You will want to paint the entire picture so that they can decide if they can handle the situation or not. Don't be afraid to ask, "Is this something/someone you feel comfortable talking with and supporting?" Acknowledge that it is a heavy situation and it's okay if it feels "too hard."

- "Pouring in" – Do they have people that pour into their lives? Do they go to counseling? Have they done the work that put them in a healthy place to help someone else? These are important things to find out when connecting them with a grieving person. Remembered, you are the buffer, so you have to protect the grieving person from more damage.

- "Listen and be Quite" – One of the main issues The Finley Project program has encountered, and I have seen in support groups is Leaders and Support people not able to lead or support without turning the relationship back on their own story. It is important when leading others to allow the space to be filled with the grieving person's pain, NOT the support person's pain. Over time, a support person can share their story, but it imperative that early on, the relationship is about the newly grieving person's story.

NOTES

_____

_____

_____

_____

_____

_____

Checklist:

Person Assigned to Find a Dedicated Support Person: _____

Dedicated Support Person's Name: _____

Introduction Made? _____

Dedicated Support Person's Contact Information: _____

Person Assigned to Schedule Weekly, Monthly & Yearly Follow-Up: _____

> " *"Kindness is the language which the deaf can hear and the blind can see."*
>
> Unknown "

NOTES

_____

_____

_____

_____

_____

_____

_____

_____

> *"I am so thankful that my dear friend Lane has never ever forgotten my Finley."*
>
>
>
> Noelle Moore, a mom who's been there

How can you and your "Core Group" continue to offer support for the months and years to follow?

There are ways you can make a grieving person feel supported long term like I did. Here are some ideas:

- LONG TERM: The Goal is to "think" LONG TERM. Often people feel forgotten after a few months, when everyone goes back to work, their lives, their friends.

- CONSISTENT: It is important to follow up CONSISTENTLY and on a regular basis, even if the person doesn't respond or say too much.

- REACH-OUT: There are way to Reach-Out. Here are some ideas:

  - Set a calendar reminder on your phone a certain day each month to send a text to the grieving person. You can say something simple: "thinking of you today."

  - Set a calendar reminder on your phone/computer to send a card every month for a year. These cards can be simple and say things like – "You and your little angel are not forgotten"; "You are Loved"…"Your precious angel loves you."

- PERSON ASSIGNED to schedule weekly, monthly, and yearly follow-up.

NOTES

_____

_____

_____

_____

_____

_____

NOTES

NOTES

Resources and Consulting

The Finley Project serves mothers in Central Florida and across the United States who have suffered stillbirth or the death of an infant from 22 weeks' gestation to 2 years of age. Our program supports mothers through the initial crisis following the loss and helps them to better manage their grief in order to reduce the long-term impact of this unique and tragic experience.

The Finley Project is the ONLY organization nationwide utilizing a holistic model to support bereaved mothers after infant loss. Our unique support program meets the practical as well as the emotional needs of mothers.

Healing is a process that takes time, so The Finley Project also continues to provide support to mothers for five years after they complete the initial program.

"What a fantastic organization! It is literally responsible for saving lives."

Dr. Anthony Orsini
Neonatologist
Founder and President of the "Orsini Way/Breaking Bad News"

"Your mothers are a testament to all that you do. I get strength from watching your amazing project. I am so honored to be a part of your mission. You make a difference every day, all in honor of sweet Finley."

Dr. Darlene Calhoun
Neonatologist

"Noelle Moore was going through some of the worst pain imaginab' , 2013: First, her father passed away while she was five months pregnant. The , medical accident during the birth led to the death of her daughter, Finley, two w s later. And two weeks after that, Moore's husband filed for divorce and ne' returned to their house.

During this period of intense grief, Moore realized tha' ,ere were very few holistic resources aimed at helping mothers get through th ,ost catastrophic stages of loss, and decided to start an organization of her own ,ich became The Finley Project." People Magazine (May 18, 2021).

Know Moore Consulting was founded by N   ,e Moore to help others know more about how to help a grieving mother. Know Moore Consulting was founded in 2014 and provides Coaching, Consulting, and Training to individuals and groups on how to help after loss using a proven Model. To learn more, please visit: www.knowmooreconsulting.com

To sign up for Weekly Reminders and tips on how to help, please go to:
www.knowmooreconsulting.com

If someone asks you what they can give to Mom...

These are ideas contributed by The Finley Program moms
of gifts they received and appreciated:

45 Thoughtful Things to Give a Grieving Mom

Jewelry

1. Necklace with child's initials
2. Locket with child picture inside
3. Angel bracelet
4. Necklace that says "Mama" or "Mom"
5. Angel wing earrings
6. Ring "angel feather"

Blankets

7. Custom quilt with child clothes
8. Custom blanket printed with child picture
9. Soft blanket (perhaps monogrammed with child's initials)

Stuffed Animals

10. Bear with heartbeat
11. Bear with ashes
12. Weighted bear
13. Stuffed animal wearing piece of child's clothing

Books/Journals

14. Journal
15. Personalized pen to go with a journal
16. Book of quotations or uplifting prayers
17. Magazines (to browse, lots of lovely photos, nature, travel spots, etc. when the grieving person isn't up to reading/focusing)
18. A gift card for books (Amazon, Barnes-N-Noble, etc)
19. Donating to the New York Public Library, which will place a customized bookplate in a book in its collection as commemoration

Other

20. "Headspace" app has a dedicated (mindfulness) program for dealing with grief (1 yr subscription)

21. Certificate of life prints

22. Ultrasound art

23. Memorial lanterns/candles

24. Garden dedication plaque

25. Soft robe & slippers

26. Bubble bath/bath bomb

27. Hot tea

28. Wind chime

29. Art showing family together

30. Christmas ornament with child's name

31. "Heaven In Our Home" engraved hurricane glass candle holder

32. Name a star. You can sponsor a star and the family gets a certificate with the child's name indicated as the official name of the star

33. Shadow box for memories/keepsakes

34. Box for keepsakes

35. Small heart-shaped stone

36. Sign for flower bed "Emma's Garden" (using the child's name)

37. Rose bush or other plant

38. Plant-a-Tree program

39. Stepping stone engraved with child's name

40. Personalized angel coffee mug (Etsy online has personalized everything)

41. Engraved photo frame

42. Embroidered pillow

43. Personalized socks

44. Original poem dedicated to the child

45. Outdoor angel statue (some have a solar light)

Know Moore Consulting educates, empowers, and coaches others on how to help after child loss – how to help others turn over a new leaf to face a new season.

Hospital Administrators, Counseling Groups, Business Owners and Others…

We appreciate you!

Contact Noelle Moore to learn how
Know Moore Consulting can help you
and your team help families
in the best way after loss.

Go to www.Knowmooreconsulting.com

and fill out the brief form.

ORDER CARE GUIDES

for your group at a SPECIAL DISCOUNT here:

www.knowmooreconsulting.com

Made in United States
Orlando, FL
06 July 2022

19459844R00046